We All Belong

by G. L. Perkins

Editorial Offices: Glenview, Illinois • Parsippany, New Jersey • New York, New York
Sales Offices: Needham, Massachusetts • Duluth, Georgia • Glenview, Illinois
Coppell, Texas • Sacramento, California • Mesa, Arizona

In our community we all belong.

We are **immigrants** from many lands.
In our community we all belong.

We speak many languages.
In our community we all belong.

ENTER
ENTREE
EINGANG
ENTRATA
ENTRADA

Welcome to the
U.S.A.
Bienvenidos a Los
Estados Unidos

POLLING PLACE
VOTE HERE

LUGAR PARA
VOTAR

VOTE AQUI

投票站

在此投票

We eat different foods.
In our community we all belong.

We have special **traditions**.
In our community we all belong.

We are all special.
In our community we all belong.

Glossary

immigrant a person who enters another
country to live there

tradition a special way that a group does
something